# Mini-Mart
## à la Carte

# Mini-Mart

## à la Carte

Christopher Rouser & Victoria Traig
Photographs by Kate Kunath

**Tasty Recipes**
for the
Convenience Store
Connoisseur!

**CHRONICLE BOOKS**

SAN FRANCISCO

Text copyright © 2005 by
Christopher Rouser and Victoria Traig

Photographs copyright © 2005 by Kate Kunath

Library of Congress Cataloging-in-Publication
Data available.

ISBN: 0-8118- 4319-X

Manufactured in China

Book and cover design by Public

Distributed in Canada by Raincoast Books
9050 Shaughnessy Street
Vancouver, British Columbia V6P 6E5

10 9 8 7 6 5 4 3 2 1

Chronicle Books LLC
85 Second Street
San Francisco, California 94105

www.chroniclebooks.com

## Dedication

**For Michaeline Rouser,
who could always do so much
with so little.**

## Acknowledgments

Our biggest thank-you goes to our co-pilot, Jennifer Traig, without whom we couldn't have written this book. Thanks to all of our families and friends who contributed ideas and tested our creations. We're indebted to Dan McGrath, Peter McGrath, Maureen and Tim Neff, Jina and Roger, KP, and Uncle D. Our gratitude to Judy and Alain Traig, whose fearless love of preservatives laid the groundwork for our future culinary endeavors. Thank you to Matt, Tanya, and Bill Rouser, for their Texas-sized love and support. We tip our hats to the entire snack food industry, and all the convenience store register jockeys across this great U.S. of A. Big thank-yous to photographer Kate Kunath and designer Public. Finally, we thank our editor Mikyla Bruder, assistant editor Leslie Davisson, and everyone else at Chronicle Books who took a chance on two kids with nothing more than a can of cheese and a dream.

# Table of Contents

# Introduction

Do you consider the mini-mart your home away from home? Do the employees at your local corner store know you by name? Do they fire up your favorite slushee when they see you coming? If the mini-mart is your safe haven in the sea of grocery stores, bakeries, and butcher shops, then you've found the only cookbook you'll ever need. *Mini-Mart à la Carte* will open the door to a world of tasty delights hiding just around the corner. Whether you call it a convenience store or mini-mart, corner store or quickie mart, it will be a beacon of light during your times of hunger and laziness. We will show you how to whip up extraordinary dishes with minimal effort, minimal cost, and maximum convenience. We will prove that there is an untapped culinary treasure trove hiding in every mini-mart. What you previously thought of as junk food can be transformed into hot, tasty, and satisfying meals. Ours is a cookbook for the self-styled mini-mart chef who values convenience as much as a hot meal. If you've got ten minutes and a mouth, this is the cookbook for you.

The following pages will dazzle you with all the nutritious and delicious dishes you can whip up from a few mini-mart staples. Perhaps you think you're getting along just fine with the microwave popcorn, chocolate milk, and Ho Hos. Maybe it is true that you can get your four basic food groups in a frozen pizza. And yes, a Hostess pie will give you enough energy until you make it to your next vending machine or fast-food joint. But what if you're invited to a potluck dinner? What if it has a Mexican theme? Well, turn to page 19 and in seven minutes you can whip up a whole platter of Pigs in a Poncho. Your friends, who assumed you'd bring a six-pack, will be floored. Or what if you met a certain special someone who likes "quiet dinners at home"? No need to panic. Just go to page 51 for our Fish Sticks Amandine or page 60 for Low Rider Lasagna. Who knows, you may be making breakfast, too (try the Rashcakes, page 94).

Don't fancy yourself much of a chef? Don't worry. It goes without saying that anyone who does all their grocery shopping at the mini-mart is not well acquainted with their kitchen appliances. We really tried to stay true to the spirit of the mini-mart by keeping everything easy. The recipes contained herein require no cooking skill and the barest minimum of tools. For the most part, the fanciest appliance you will need to make any of these recipes is a can opener. Many of them can, in fact, be prepared using only the mini-mart's microwave and coffee bar. So if you don't own a microwave and you have your heart set on the Chef Boyardee Blitzkrieg (page 55), just bring a bowl and your can opener with you and nuke it right there in the oven in the store. That's what it's there for.

For you gourmet types who are more familiar with food served *en croûte* than on a stick, we have some things for you, too. It may seem that this cookbook is geared only to those who are a little more laid-back with their cooking style. *Au contraire, mon frère. Mini-Mart à la Carte* is also a kitchen companion to you fancy folk who are looking to expand your horizons—to lower your brow, but not your wow.

We start you off small, with a chapter devoted to appetizers, snacks, and side dishes. These are munchies that are small in size, but huge in character, bouquet, and taste. Why reach for a candy bar to keep you merely (ahem) satisfied, when you could whip up a batch of Nutty Sombrero (page 22) and be fulfilled? If you are pressed for time, and the only heat source available is the light that radiates from your smile, you can have a delicious and nutritious Frito Boat (page 26) in a matter of seconds. Don't give in to those same tired snacks when you can feed your soul with a genuine mini-mart nugget, one that will give you the push that you need to help you through your day. It's all smooth sailing from here.

Once your taste buds have been tickled and your appetite has been aroused, you'll be ready for the chapter on main courses. We'll show you how to cook up everything from seafood to pastas, breakfasts to kabobs, all with the flair of a seasoned mini-mart chef. These treats aren't just salty; they're sultry. They are not merely tasty; they're double tasty. Who can resist such elegant edibles as SPAM Wellington (page 47) or Tuna on a Cloud (page 62)? Not you. In fact, those of you who never seem to finish a whole meal before becoming bored might want to splurge on a pair of elastic pants, because your underfed belly is finally going to get the workout it deserves.

In Chapter 3, we dive head first into the sea of mini-mart quaffs. Beverages are more than just a way to prevent dehydration; they mark times and events. We drink coffee in the morning, sodas during the day, and cocktails at night. We drink Champagne to celebrate special events. Drinks can make or break a mood, and mini-marts always offer a bevy of beverages. Who could be down in the dumps while sipping on a bubbly Mickey Rourke cooler (page 80)? We know thirst can be a complicated thing, and often a "one-trick pony" like orange juice or wine doesn't satisfy it. At your next cocktail party you'll look smart and sophisticated holding a tall glass of the Pink of Health (page 82). While your friends are all waiting in line for the porcelain god, your belly will be good as gold, coated with this drink's nausea-fighting secret ingredient.

If you find that your sweet tooth is the ruler of your mouth, your head, and your heart, look no further than the desserts in Chapter 4 to quell your desires. Just as there is an appropriate time for everything, there are appropriate times to satisfy your lust for sweets. We recommend: before and after dinner, for dinner, lunch, and breakfast, while smoking, after sex, instead of sex, at work, while watching TV, during your bath, before yoga, during a sporting event, and in between the hours in which you wake up and go to sleep. Now, with all these time slots needing to be filled with a sugary snack, surely you would become bored with the same thirty or so candy bars on the market. You have adventurous tastes, and besides, candy bars are so seventies. We know that you're also busy, and don't always have the time or money to bake a Bundt cake or pecan pie. We feel your pain and we've got a prescription for you: a heaping bowl of Banana Nicole Smith (page 91). And if that doesn't work we've got loads of other reasons for you to feed the Snickers to the dog and whip yourself up a real treat.

We bet you've already got a little drool trickling down your chin right now. So what are you waiting for? It's time to arm yourself with a can of Cheez Whiz, some SPAM, and a 40-ounce bottle of malt liquor. A whole world of convenience store cuisine awaits you. Invite some friends, your parents, or a date or two, and go to town. On second thought, don't. You'll never have to go to town again—just to the mini-mart.

# THE MINI-MART QUIZ

Before we take the next step, we should define exactly what we consider a mini-mart.
Just take this little quiz to find out whether your favorite store is a mini-mart or an impostor.
Answer yes or no:

1. Does it have only one entrance that does not open automatically?
2. Are the windows plastered with cigarette posters and/or advertisements for dangerously cheap hot dogs?
3. Is there a self-serve dispenser for artificially flavored frozen fruit drinks?
4. Can you walk around the store in less than 50 paces?
5. Is there usually an employee outside smoking a cigarette?
6. Can you check your hair in the security cameras?
7. Is Miller Genuine Draft the highest-priced beer in stock?
8. Is the red wine chilled?
9. Is there a gas pump?
10. Do the magazines with covers featuring naked women and/or fast cars outnumber the rest of the magazines combined?

If you answered yes seven or more times, congratulations, your corner store is indeed a mini-mart!

# HOW TO USE THIS BOOK

Basically, the ingredients for every recipe that follows should be available in the quintessential mini-mart. However, this book is as much a guide to mini-mart culture as it is a cookbook. Each chapter contains mini-mart craft projects, dinner party ideas, and helpful tips; lessons in mini-mart etiquette; and historical tidbits and topical trivia, along with the recipes, to create not just a meal, but a whole mini-mart experience.

To further enhance the experience, we've coded some recipes with symbols:

**!** Recipes with this symbol fall into the **At Your Own Risk** category. While there is no danger of illness or injury, these recipes are not for the faint of heart, vanilla-only ice cream eaters, hypochondriacs, neurotics, nongamblers, pregnant women, or the elderly. If you were the first kid on your block to fly down a hill on a bike with no brakes, or the first in your family to break a bone, then these recipes will definitely pique your interest. Creative ingredient combinations are the cornerstones of these recipes, which are tailor-made for the bold mini-mart chef who never shies away from a dare. They're our version of an extreme sport.

**✳** Recipes with this symbol can be made entirely in the mini-mart using their appliances (though you may have to omit a simple step for the in-store job, such as toasting a bun). For most of these recipes you will need to bring some simple cooking equipment from home, though usually just a plastic bowl or a can opener.

**1**

Appetizers,
Snacks,
and Sides

Maybe an appetizer is just what you need to get a party off on the right foot, or maybe you just need a little something to keep you going through that midday hump or those pesky midnight cravings. Either way, you do not want to allow your culinary sensibilities to suffer. Now, the ignorant would argue that you should just hoof it down to the corner store, pick up a bag of chips, and get on with it. But the enlightened eye sees those same chips as pieces of a bigger, more beautiful puzzle that can be put together in haste, if need be, but in great taste, as must-be. These are snacks with a capital S, hors d'oeuvres with a capital O. Whether as the first step on the stairway to mini-mart heaven or a delicious jump-start along your busy day, these little recipes will always make a big impression.

APR 06
700795

# *Chicken Wings* CORDON BLEU

If you can't decide which you love more, American food or French, this snack is for you. It's a delicious Parisian delicacy wrapped in an American flag. Sliced ham and American cheese cloak fried chicken wings to create a mouth-watering treat that's good down to the bone. It's soul food on a stick! It's a poultry candy apple! It's Eurotrash you can eat!

*You will need:*

**One 16-ounce package frozen chicken wings (16 wings)**

**8 slices ham, cut in quarters lengthwise**

**4 slices American cheese singles, cut in quarters lengthwise**

Preheat the oven to 400 degrees F.

Place the chicken wings on an ungreased baking sheet and bake for 18 minutes.

Remove from the oven and lay 2 slices of ham on top of each chicken wing. Lay 1 strip of cheese on top of each ham duo.

Bake until the cheese is thoroughly melted, about 5 minutes longer. Serve hot.

**SERVES 4 EXPATRIATES**

# *The Mini-Mart* FOOD PYRAMID

**FRESH PRODUCE:**
lemons, onions

**BEVERAGES:**
slushees, soda, malt liquor

**CANNED FOODS:**
beans, SpaghettiOs, chili

**SALTY SNACKS:**
chips, nuts, crackers,
popcorn

**SWEETS:**
candy bars, taffy, donuts,
Twinkies

**PROCESSED MEATS:**
SPAM, Vienna sausages, salami, jerky

# The RANCHY Conquistador *

Ahoy, all you adventurers who consider ranch to be the holy grail of flavor! Plot yourselves a course through the hidden valley to this uncharted treat. Will waves of ranchy *queso* capsize the crunch of the Cooler Ranch! Doritos? There are no guarantees on the high seas of flavor, friend.

*You will need:*

**One 3 1/2-ounce bag Cooler Ranch! Doritos**

**1 cup spicy cheese dip, such as Tostitos salsa con queso**

**One 8-ounce bottle ranch dressing**

Spread the chips evenly on a large serving plate.

In a small microwave-safe bowl, heat the spicy cheese dip in the microwave oven on high for about 3 minutes, or until heated throughout.

Pour the cheese dip evenly over the chips.

Pour the ranch dressing evenly over the cheesy chips and serve.

**SERVES 4**

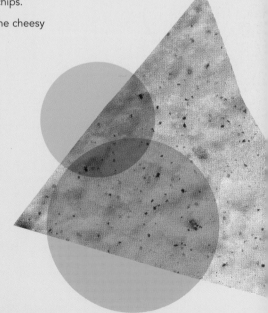

¡Olé!

# Pigs in a PONCHO ✳

This little piggy went to market, this little piggy stayed home. And this little piggy hopped into his souped–up low rider and headed to Tijuana. We've nestled our little piggies under a blanket of cheese sauce and wrapped them snugly in a tortilla comforter. And for a pillow, how about some hot sauce? This little piggy went wee, wee, wee all the way to your belly.

*You will need:*

**One 16-ounce package hot dogs**

**8 taco-sized soft flour tortillas**

**One 8-ounce can Cheddar-flavor Kraft Easy Cheese**

**1 packet taco sauce from the condiment bar**

Place the hot dogs on a microwave-safe plate and heat in the microwave oven on high for about 4 minutes, or until the dogs are heated throughout.

Place each hot dog on a tortilla and spray liberally with Easy Cheese.

Wrap the tortillas snugly around the hot dogs.

Squirt the taco sauce in a thick line on a large serving platter, arrange the piggies in a row along the line of sauce, and serve.

**SERVES 4 PIGGIES**

## MICROWAVING AT HIGH ALTITUDES

Unlike baking, where a change of altitude can affect cooking times, the miracle that is the microwave heats things up in the same amount of time whether you are in the bowels of the Grand Canyon or perched high atop Mount McKinley. Still, there are some precautions one should take when microwaving at higher altitudes:

1. **Don't smoke.** You're already getting less oxygen and that combined with the nicotine will likely make you light-headed.

2. **Don't stand up too fast.** Again, you will likely get light-headed.

3. **Don't wear tight shoes.** Feet tend to swell up at higher elevations, and tight shoes could become unbearably uncomfortable, cutting off circulation and causing irrational thoughts, such as going to an organic grocery store.

# *New England* SPAM CHOWDER

You spent a long day on the lake paddling your inflatable raft up and down the shore. Now it's time to eat, and you want something befitting the salty dog you are. Something warm and hearty like clam chowder. Don't let the fact that you live in Minnesota and the closest clam is two thousand miles away get you down. Make your chowder with something just as unkosher: spiced pork!

*You will need:*

**One 12-ounce can SPAM**

**One 10 1/2-ounce can cream of potato soup**

**One 10 1/2-ounce can cream of celery soup**

**1 1/2 cups milk**

**1/4 teaspoon pepper**

**1/2 cup instant mashed potato flakes**

Cut the SPAM into 1/2-inch dice and fry in a skillet over medium heat until crispy. Transfer to paper towels to drain.

In a saucepan, mix both cans of soup with the milk and heat until simmering.

Add the pepper and potato flakes to the soups and stir until dissolved.

Stir in the SPAM and serve.

**SERVES 4**

# The NUTTY Sombrero ✳

Here's the situation: You just Mexican–Hat–Danced your ass off and now you are *muy* hungry. Chips and salsa sounds good, sure, but you need a little more substance. Try adding a blast of fat and flavor to your salsa with peanut butter. You'll be glad you did. And everywhere you go you'll find yourself singing that traditional Mexican tune: "Whether it's Cinco de Mayo or Uno de Enero, It's never a bad time for the Nutty Sombrero."

*You will need:*

**One 16-ounce jar salsa**

**1 cup chunky peanut butter**

**$^1/_3$ cup lemon juice**

**One 13$^1/_2$-ounce bag tortilla chips**

Pour, scoop, and squeeze the salsa, peanut butter, and lemon juice into a bowl.

Stir until the peanut butter dissolves into the salsa and the mixture is well combined.

Serve with the tortilla chips.

**SERVES 4 CABALLEROS**

# GETTING A FOOT IN THE DOOR

A good tactic to ensure complete flexibility with your mini-mart experience is to get "in" with at least one of the clerks. Most of these folks
keep regular schedules, so you can time your trips to the store to corre-
spond with a favorite employee's shift. Let them get to know your face,
and then start calling them by name. Give them a nickname, something
slangy, like "S-Dog" or "Super P." Compliment them on haircuts and
changes in style ("That upturned collar sure makes your neck look thick!").
Pretty soon, you'll have the rule of the roost, able to whip up a three-
course in-store meal with not so much as a sour look in your direction. In
addition, always offer some of the booty to the clerk. He probably won't
accept, but your kindness will definitely be noted and appreciated.

# *Saucy* DEVILS

This appetizer is a cholesterol–lover's dream come true. We've added deviled ham to deviled eggs to create a sinful snack that is not for the faint of heart. Your tummy will thank us; your cardiologist will curse us.

*You will need:*

**FOR THE DEVILED EGGS**

8 eggs

2 packets mayonnaise from the condiment bar

2 tablespoons deviled ham spread

**FOR THE SAUCE**

2 packets mayonnaise from the condiment bar

2 packets ketchup from the condiment bar

To make the deviled eggs, in a saucepan, cover the eggs with cold water and bring to a boil over high heat. Reduce the heat to a simmer and cook the eggs for 15 minutes.

Drain the hot water and add fresh cold water; let stand until the eggs have cooled.

Peel the cooled eggs and cut each in half lengthwise. Remove the yolks and place them in a small bowl. Add the mayonnaise and deviled ham and mix well. Spoon the yolk mixture back into the egg white halves.

To make the sauce, stir the mayonnaise and ketchup together in a small bowl. Drizzle onto the deviled egg halves and serve.

**SERVES 4**

## UNCLE JOHNNY'S MINI-MART HISTORY MINUTE

In 1927, a visionary, hero, and pioneer by the name of John Jefferson "Uncle Johnny" Green opened the first convenience store in the world. His shop, Southland Ice Company, originally stocked only ice until Uncle Johnny, a shrewd businessman and a true genius, saw that his business and his community both would benefit from the sale of a few basic grocery items like milk, cheese, and bread, available seven days a week, sixteen hours a day. And thus, the world was forever changed and the mini-mart was born.

# *Frito* Boat  !

All hands on deck, and prepare to board the mighty Frito Boat setting sail for a brave new world. Brave, indeed, as this tasty little morsel is as much a snack as it is an adventure. This is a dish that requires equal parts hunger and daring. First you must buy the Fritos, then quickly slice open the bag and dump loads of free hot dog chili onto the chips before the clerk realizes what you are doing. For once, having all that empty space in a bag of chips comes in handy!

*You will need:*

**One 2³/₄-ounce bag Fritos**

**Pocketknife, scissors, or other cutting tool**

**Access to free hot dog chili**

**Balls of steel**

Pay for the Fritos, then discreetly cut open the bag on a side seam, rather than the top or bottom. Deftly and inconspicuously heap free hot dog chili into the bag.

Make your escape. Enjoy your hearty snack and the satisfaction of having pulled it off.

**SERVES 1**

# Notzoh Ball Soup

Some people complain that mini-marts have little to no specialty food items. No international foods, no health foods, and certainly no kosher foods. To those people we say, "Oy Vey! Stop your kvetching already!" While it's true that most mini-marts don't carry any Manischewitz products, they do carry a wide variety of other staples that, when mixed together correctly, can create scrumptious exotic foods, such as this kosher facsimile. *L'Chaim!*

*You will need:*

**2 eggs**

**2 teaspoons vegetable oil**

**2 teaspoons water**

**24 Ritz crackers, smashed into a fine meal**

**Pinch each of salt and pepper**

**Two 14-ounce cans chicken broth**

In a bowl, lightly beat the eggs with a fork. Add the vegetable oil, water, cracker meal, and salt and pepper. Refrigerate for 15 minutes.

In a large saucepan, bring the chicken broth to a slow boil.

Roll the batter into quarter-sized balls and add to the boiling broth. Simmer gently until the notzoh balls are cooked throughout, about 30 minutes. Serve immediately.

**SERVES 4**

# The TROJAN Horse !

This work of art is both an appetizer and a centerpiece. A horse-shaped SPAM shell hides a tasty invasion of Velveeta cheese. Defeat never tasted so good.

*You will need:*

**One 12-ounce can SPAM**

**2 ounces Velveeta cheese, cut into $^1/_2$-inch cubes**

**1 toothpick**

Preheat the oven to 425 degrees F.

Basically, you're going to carve up the hunk of SPAM into a horse shape.

To make the legs: Unpack the SPAM, drain, and pat dry on paper towels. Lay the hunk flat with a long side facing you. Cutting through the entire thickness of the SPAM, cut out a square about 2 inches long and $^1/_2$ inch deep from the center of the long side; set aside this piece for the head. Then cut a $^3/_4$-inch square out of the middle of both of the short sides to form the four legs.

To prepare the body for cheese hiding, turn the form over and rest it on its legs. Gently slice a $^1/_2$-inch thick piece of SPAM off the top; this is the lid. Using a knife and a spoon, carve out the inside, leaving the walls and bottom about $^1/_2$-inch thick. Work carefully to avoid breaking the sides or legs.

Fill the hollow of the SPAM horse with the Velveeta chunks. Replace the lid.

To make the head: Slice the reserved square of SPAM in half and discard one half. Detail the remaining half with eyes, a mouth, and a mane and secure horizontally where a head ought to be on top of the lid, using the toothpick. (Don't forget to craft a tail!)

Place the Trojan horse in a shallow baking pan and bake until the cheese is melted and the SPAM is sizzling and starting to crisp, about 10 minutes. Serve hot.

**SERVES AN ARMY (AN ARMY OF 4 PEOPLE)**

Mini-Mart Craft Project

## SPAM SCULPTURE 101

Spam is such a versatile product. Not only is it a tasty and salty meat with which to make any variety of meals, but it's also a splendid medium for creating art. It's thick, but not heavy. It's smooth, but not greasy. Start by carving out simple shapes, like toy cars and your initials, with a kitchen knife. When you're feeling more confident, move on to houses and flowers. Finally, try sculpting a self-portrait.

# POOP on a Pringle ✳

What we have here is a PG–13 version of an old military standby. Everyone, from kids who like to play war to grizzled old army vets, will get a kick out of these salty snacks. Plus, we guarantee that mess hall duty will never be this easy. Charge!

Lay out the Pringles on a large serving plate.

Spread a scant tablespoon of bean dip on each Pringle.

Cut the Vienna sausages into thirds and place 1 piece in the middle of each chip. (Eat the last piece of Vienna sausage.) Serve your country—your party, that is.

**SERVES 4**

*You will need:*

**20 original-flavor Pringles**

**One 9-ounce can bean dip**

**One 5-ounce can Vienna sausages (7 sausages)**

# PLEASED TO MEAT YOU:
# A HISTORICAL NOTE FOR MEAT LOVERS

Processed meats are the cornerstones of any mini-mart. But most of us take for granted how easy it is to get a meaty snack on the go these days. Back in the day, the process of getting a good slab of meat in hand or to the dinner table was a painfully long (and sometimes dangerous) affair. First, a person had to fashion a crude weapon out of a stick. Then, they had to travel many miles and wait many moons for their prey. Some hunters would get trampled by buffalo. Some would succumb to friendly fire, and head back home with a spear in the neck. Others would stub their toe and limp back to the cave, dejected. Once the quarry was caught, the arduous journey back began. Upon returning, a fire had to be made using two rocks and a spark that never seemed to catch.

Nowadays, thanks to the technological advances of the twentieth century and the invention of preservatives, all you have to do to procure some satisfying meat is stroll to the corner, slap down some cash, and peel off the plastic. Straight from the farm to the mini-mart (with maybe a few stops in between), processed meats cure hunger like nobody's business. The best part: You don't have to worry about any pesky expiration dates.

# **Sardines** Rockefeller

With this canapé we honor the golden age that was fifties' enter-
taining: Imagine housewives with beehives in their pristine
aprons, serving old-fashioneds and ritzy hors d'oeuvres. Here is
an appetizer that lets your guests know you're one classy host.
We've eliminated the one wild card in this deck: the oyster. We
don't know about you, but we don't like to play seafood roulette
with our bellies. The sardine is the perfect substitute—it's less
slimy and cuter to look at.

*You will need:*

$^3/_4$ **cup drained
canned spinach,
finely chopped**

$^1/_4$ **cup crushed
original-flavor
Pringles**

**1 tablespoon Bac-Os**

$^1/_2$ **teaspoon, plus
1 cup salt**

**2 drops Tabasco**

**1 tablespoon butter,
softened**

**12 Ritz crackers**

**Three 3$^3/_4$-ounce tins
sardines**

Preheat the oven to 450 degrees F.

In a small bowl, combine the spinach, Pringles, Bac-Os, the
$^1/_2$ teaspoon salt, and Tabasco. Add the butter and stir to
mix well.

Place the crackers on a baking sheet. Patting each sardine
dry on paper towels as you remove it from the tin, top each
cracker with 1 sardine. Top with a heaping teaspoon of the
spinach mixture.

Bake for 10 minutes, or until the crackers have browned
a shade darker. Let cool.

Spread 1 cup salt on a serving platter to depth of about
$^3/_4$ inch. When the canapés are cool enough to handle,
arrange them on the salt.

Put on your high heels, tease your hair, and serve.

# Carny's *Delight*

Ah, the wonders of summer: sun, fun, and a barrage of fairs and carnivals. And what is the most memorable aspect of those dreamy festivals? Is it the swirling rides, the cotton candy, the games? Or is it the scraggly, toothless man whistling at you as you pass the Tilt-o-Whirl? This hearty side dish is in honor of those working-class men who made our childhood summers so memorable.

Preheat the oven to 425 degrees F.

In a saucepan, bring 6 cups of water to a boil. Add the macaroni and cook until tender, 10–12 minutes.

Drain the macaroni and return it to the saucepan. Stir in the butter, milk, and cheese sauce packet.

De-stick the corn dogs and slice into 1-inch chunks.

Transfer the macaroni and cheese to a greased 1¹/₂-quart casserole dish. Stir in the corn dog bites. Top with the french fried onions and bake for 15 minutes, or until the onions are golden brown and crispy. Serve hot.

**SERVES 4**

*You will need:*

**One 7¹/₄-ounce package macaroni and cheese mix**

**¹/₄ cup butter or margarine, softened**

**¹/₂ cup milk**

**2 corn dogs from the mini-mart's fried-food case (if you're unlucky enough to live next to the one mini-mart that still doesn't have a fried-food case, you can substitute frozen corn dogs)**

**³/₄ cup French's french fried onions**

# Corn-a-Plenty CHOWDER ✳

This recipe is an eye–opener for all you folks who haven't yet real-
ized what culinary magic awaits you when you reap the harvests
of canned goods. In this delicate soup we combine creamed corn
and tomatoes—so simple, so elegant—to make a first course that
will make your taste buds sing.

*You will need:*

**One 15-ounce can
creamed corn**

**One 14 1/2-ounce can
crushed tomatoes**

In a microwave-safe bowl, combine the corn and tomatoes.
Heat in the microwave oven on high for 4–5 minutes, or
until heated throughout.

Ladle the soup into 2 bowls and serve.

**SERVES 2**

# MINI-MART ETIQUETTE

A note on in-store cooking: As with most things in life, there is an appropriate time and place for everything. If you are a first-time customer and the mini-mart is having its after-school candy rush, it would probably be inappropriate to prepare a meal in-store. We recommend that you are well acquainted with and well liked by the staff of a mini-mart before you attempt any in-store cooking. Use your best judgment and follow your instincts. Figure out in advance what the pros and cons are for preparing a certain dish in-store versus at home. Are you on your way to a monster truck rally? Preparing a meal in-store makes sense so you won't have to stop back home to eat. Are you on your way home from a motocross race? Prepare at home then, so you won't have to remember to bring a can opener.

# Ramen *Romanoff*

Noodles Romanoff is a dairy–lover's dream come true. Its bounty of noodles, cheese, and sour cream makes boxed macaroni and cheese looks like child's play. As is our style, we've added special mini–mart flair by substituting sleek and slippery ramen noodles for boring old egg noodles to make a side dish that will jazz up any entrée.

In a saucepan, bring 3 cups of water to a boil. Add the noodles and cook until tender, about 3 minutes.

Drain the noodles and return them to the saucepan. Place over medium heat and add the cottage cheese, sour cream, and salt. Stir to mix well.

Transfer the noodle mixture to a bowl, sprinkle with the Cheddar cheese, and serve.

**SERVES 4**

*You will need:*

**Two 3-ounce packages ramen noodles**

**$1/_2$ cup cottage cheese**

**$1/_2$ cup sour cream**

**$1/_4$ teaspoon salt**

**$1/_2$ cup shredded Cheddar cheese**

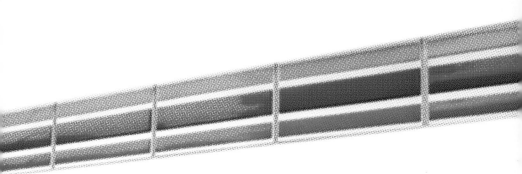

## MINI-MART TRIVIA

In 2002, mini-mart chain 7-Eleven sold thirty-three million gallons of fountain drinks. That's enough liquid to fill over seventy-five Olympic-sized swimming pools.

# The Kevin **BACON** ✳

Now you can trim those six degrees of Kevin Bacon down to one by bringing the versatile actor into your dining room. With lots of cheese to wrap itself around, it's the perfect role for bacon, and it definitely rewards repeated eatings. Kenny Loggins soundtrack not included.

*You will need:*

**24 ounces cream cheese**

**1 photo of Kevin Bacon**

**One 4-ounce jar Bac-Os**

**Crackers of your choice**

Dump all the cream cheese into a large bowl and smash it into a ball.

Using your photo for reference, sculpt the cheese into a likeness of Kevin Bacon.

Pour the Bac-Os onto a plate and gently roll Kevin Bacon's head around until he is evenly coated with bits. You may have to sprinkle some on to cover exposed spaces. Press gently all over to make the bits adhere.

Serve Kevin Bacon's head on a platter, with crackers.

**SERVES 12**

### Variation: Bacon's Balls

*Nonartists can simply roll the cream cheese into 3-inch balls, coat with the bacon bits, and serve.*

# Wiener Bean Bucket ✳

No truly honest person can deny the allure of franks and beans. Sure, some of your friends may claim that their tastes are more sophisticated, but really, who are they kidding? Here we've crammed together loads of hot dogs and baked beans to warm even the most sophisticated belly. If you're really worried that your friends are too chic for this dish, just tell them it's foie gras. No one really knows what that is anyway.

*You will need:*

**Two 15 ³/₄-ounce cans pork and beans**

**¹/₃ cup ketchup**

**¹/₄ cup water**

**2 tablespoons brown sugar**

**1 packet yellow mustard from the condiment bar**

**8 hot dogs, cut into 1-inch chunks**

In a 2-quart microwave-safe casserole dish, combine the beans, ketchup, water, brown sugar, mustard, and hot dogs. Stir to mix well and cover.

Heat in the microwave oven on high until heated throughout, 8–10 minutes. Serve hot.

**SERVES 6**

# Main
# Courses

The main course is the "meat" of the mini-mart experience. It can make you or break you. It will ask you to prom or kick you to the curb. To the amateur gourmet, these recipes might seem a little daunting, as some even require both hands to count all the ingredients. But do not fret, fledgling chef, just think of these recipes as confidence builders. And once you have built one of these mini-mart entrées from scratch, there will be no stopping you, barring some unforeseen catastrophic event that causes all mini-marts to close their doors.

If you are a practiced chef and are skeptical about the mini-mart cooking movement, or are a card-carrying member of the so-called "grocery store cult," prepare to be converted. One taste of, say, Tuna Sasserole (page 44), and you will already be planning your next convenience-store culinary adventure. Have a tasty trip!

# Eggs Benedict Arnold

It's true. We're traitors. Traitors to the poached egg. Traitors to Hollandaise sauce. But by substituting scrambled for poached eggs and adding the zing of nacho cheese, we feel like patriots— patriots of taste. And we're sure that ol' Benedict never would have sold out his country had he started off with this delicious breakfast on that fateful day.

In a small bowl, beat together the eggs and milk.

Pour the egg mixture into a greased frying pan over medium heat and cook until the eggs are soft curds and opaque throughout.

Cut the bagels in half and toast in a toaster until golden brown.

Pour the cheese dip into a microwave-safe bowl. Heat in the microwave oven on high until heated throughout, about 30 seconds.

Divide the eggs among the bagel halves, heaping them on top. Pour 2 tablespoons hot cheese dip atop each egged bagel and serve.

**SERVES 2**

*You will need:*

**4 eggs**

**¹/₄ cup milk**

**2 bagels**

**¹/₂ cup nacho cheese dip such as Tostitos salsa con queso**

## UNCLE JOHNNY'S MINI-MART HISTORY MINUTE

The end of World War II, along with an increase in car ownership, led to a convenience-store boom during the 1950s. People moved out to the suburbs where there was more space, and therefore more space in between grocery stores. Mini-marts began popping up in neighborhoods too small to sustain a supermarket.

# Tuna *Sasserole*

You're hip. You're sassy. You don't like boiling noodles that don't come with their own flavor packet. This dish is for you, Miss Thang. Chicken of the sea collides with ramen noodles to create a meal that's reminiscent of your mom's makeshift casseroles but even easier to make. This is a meal you can serve to your most mature friends without betraying your youthful sensibilities.

Preheat the oven to 375 degrees F.

In a saucepan, bring 3 cups of water to a boil. Break up the ramen noodles and add to the boiling water. Cook until tender, about 3 minutes.

Drain the noodles and return to the saucepan. Add the milk, soup, peas, tuna, and flavor packet. Stir to mix well.

Transfer the noodle mixture to a 1¹/₂-quart greased casserole dish. Top with the Cheddar cheese and crushed potato chips. Bake, uncovered, until heated throughout, about 30 minutes. Serve hot.

**SERVES 6**

*You will need:*

**Three 3-ounce packages ramen noodles**

**³/₄ cup milk**

**One 10¹/₂-ounce can cream of mushroom soup**

**One 8¹/₂-ounce can sweet peas**

**Two 6-ounce cans tuna**

**1 flavor packet from the ramen noodles**

**2 ounces Cheddar cheese, sliced or grated**

**One 2³/₄-ounce bag potato chips, crushed (see page 61)**

# Chipped Pizza

Nothing says "gourmet" quite like a handmade pizza on homemade crust. We've forgone that annoying rustic wood-fired business for a pie that's more in tune with our mini-mart sensibilities: pizza on potato chip crust. We've topped our Idaho-Italy hybrid with pepperoni jerky bits, but you're welcome to add salami, ham, or even a can of corn to create a pie that's custom-made to your tastes.

Preheat the oven to 350 degrees F.

In a large bowl, combine the chips and eggs and stir to mix well.

Line a baking sheet with greased waxed paper and dump the potato chip dough in the middle. Using your hands, shape the dough into an 8-inch circle.

Bake for about 15 minutes, or until the crust starts to feel firm.

Remove from the oven and top with the tomato sauce, string cheese, and jerky. Return to the oven and bake until the cheese is melted, about 5 minutes or longer.

Cut the pie into 6 slices and serve.

**SERVES 6**

*You will need:*

**Two 2³/₄-ounce bags Lay's classic potato chips, crushed (see page 61)**

**3 eggs, lightly beaten**

**¹/₄ cup tomato sauce**

**Six 1-ounce string cheese sticks, ripped into small strings**

**1 stick pepperoni-flavored beef jerky, cut into bite-sized morsels**

## A NOTE TO VEGETARIANS

Flipping through this book, you will find a wide
variety of foods that you can't, or won't, eat.
Unfortunately, this leaves you with only one option.
Start eating meat! Now, it might be a little rough
on your intestines at first, but in a couple of weeks,
we assure you that will iron itself out. Good luck,
and above all, enjoy!

MEAT

# SPAM Wellington

Of all the recipes in this book, we consider this to be our magnum opus. Gourmet and greasy, it's what all mini-mart cuisine aspires to be. Golden Bisquick pastry cloaks a roast of SPAM and a thin layer of mini-mart pâté (deviled ham). Serve this to your most discerning friends, who can appreciate a delicate yet wholly satisfying repast.

Preheat the oven to 425 degrees F.

In a bowl, combine the Bisquick, egg yolk, water, and oil with a fork. Mix well and form into a ball. Refrigerate for 20 minutes.

Meanwhile, place the whole SPAM on a small pie plate and bake for 10 minutes. Remove from the oven and set aside. Leave the oven on.

Meanwhile, place the chilled dough on a lightly floured work surface and roll into an 11-by-14-inch rectangle.

Spread the deviled ham onto the pastry and place the heated SPAM in the center. Carefully wrap your SPAM like the gift that it is, covering it entirely in the dough. Place the dough-wrapped SPAM seam side down on a greased baking sheet.

In a small bowl, beat the egg white. Brush the egg white all over the pastry. Bake until the pastry is golden brown, about 10 minutes.

Slice into 1-inch-thick pieces. Serve with the A1 sauce.

**SERVES 6**

*You will need:*

**1 1/2 cups original Bisquick**

**1 egg, separated**

**4 tablespoons cold water**

**2 tablespoons vegetable oil**

**One 12-ounce can SPAM**

**One 4 1/4-ounce can deviled ham spread**

**One bottle A1 Steak Sauce**

# Bat out of Hell Meatloaf !

First, an entertainer names himself after a dinner, then the dinner comes right back in his face and reclaims the name, along with the singer's album title. At least that's what happened here with our ketchup-glazed corned beef hash meatloaf. It's the oldest rivalry on record between a rock star and a meat dish, but the ironic thing is that these two have so much in common: thick, meaty, and surprisingly enjoyable.

Preheat the oven to 350 degrees F.

In a large bowl, combine the egg, milk, crackers, onions, ketchup, mustard, salt, and pepper. Stir to mix well. Add the hash and stir to combine roughly.

Transfer the hash mixture to a greased 7½-by-3½-inch loaf pan. Cover with aluminum foil and bake for 30 minutes.

Meanwhile, make the glaze: In a bowl, stir together the ketchup, mustard, and brown sugar.

Remove the meatloaf from the oven and remove the foil from the pan. Pour the glaze over the meatloaf and spread to coat evenly. Return to the oven and bake for 30 minutes longer, for a total cooking time of 1 hour. Let stand for 10 minutes, then cut into 1-inch-thick slices and serve.

**SERVES 6**

*You will need:*

**FOR THE MEATLOAF**

1 egg, lightly beaten

⅓ cup milk

24 Ritz crackers, crushed

1 handful diced onions from the condiment bar

1 packet ketchup from the condiment bar

1 packet mustard from the condiment bar

½ teaspoon salt

¼ teaspoon pepper

One 15-ounce can corned beef hash

**FOR THE GLAZE**

⅓ cup ketchup

1 packet mustard from the condiment bar

3 tablespoons brown sugar

## THE WONDERS OF ALUMINUM FOIL

Unless you're a newlywed, you likely don't have a wide variety of baking dishes and pans. Don't let your limited supply of cooking gear dictate what you can and cannot make, not when you've got at your disposal the handiest custom pan-shaper ever: aluminum foil. All you need is one large baking dish, and with that you can construct foil walls to custom-fit any recipe requirements. Just take a large sheet of foil, smash it down, and cram it into place. It's that easy.

# Fish Sticks *Amandine*

Do you love fish sticks but feel they might be a little too third grade for a dinner party? Are you sick of your friends snickering behind your back as you dive headlong into a plate of golden fishy goodness? Here's a way to put an end to their snobbery. This delicate entrée dresses up your favorite snack sticks in a sleek almond sauce that's sure to impress folks of all ages with even the most sophisticated of palates.

Preheat the oven to 400 degrees F.

Place the fish sticks on an ungreased baking sheet and bake until crispy, 18–22 minutes.

Meanwhile, in a frying pan over medium heat, melt the butter. Add the almonds and sauté until golden brown, about 5 minutes.

Place the fish sticks on a large platter, spoon the butter and almond mixture on top, and serve.

**SERVES 4**

*You will need:*

**One 11.4-ounce package frozen fish sticks (16 fish sticks)**

**$1/_4$ cup butter or margarine**

**$1/_4$ cup sliced almonds**

# PIMP'S Pie

In the days of yore, shepherds would spend their days herding their flock and tending to their every need. This was grueling work, and at the end of the day they would sup on hearty meals such as shepherd's pie. This update of the dish gives a nod to the shepherd of today: the pimp. He tends to his little lambs much the same way, while managing to elude Johnny Law at the same time. This recipe is a quickie, but very satisfying.

*You will need:*

**One 15-ounce can no-bean chili con carne**

**One 14 1/2-ounce can cut green beans**

**One 10 3/4-ounce can tomato soup**

**3/4 cup milk**

**1 1/2 cups water**

**1 2/3 cups instant mashed potato flakes**

**2 ounces Cheddar cheese, sliced or grated**

Preheat the oven to 425 degrees F.

In a greased 1 1/2-quart casserole dish, combine the chili, green beans, and soup. Stir to mix well.

In a microwave-safe bowl, combine the milk and water and heat in the microwave oven on high until the liquid is hot, about 2 minutes.

Stir the potato flakes into the milk mixture, then spoon on top of the chili mixture. Sprinkle evenly with the Cheddar cheese. Bake, uncovered, until heated throughout, about 30 minutes.

Don your favorite fedora, polyester pantsuit, and platform shoes and enjoy!

**SERVES 4**

# Chili con **Corne** ✳

This is another in our series of "Open two cans, you've got a meal" recipes (see Corn-a-Plenty Chowder, page 34). Open one can and you're lazy. But open two cans and voilà, you are a bona fide chef. This corn-rich recipe is great for those vegetable-phobes who need a little fiber. No vegetable is less vegetably than corn! Plus, corn makes things look fancy. Corn in salsa = fancy. Corn in chili = fancy and yummy.

In a microwave-safe bowl, combine the chili and corn and stir to mix well. Heat in the microwave oven on high until heated throughout, 4–5 minutes.

Ladle the chili into 2 bowls and chow down.

**SERVES 2**

*You will need:*

**One 15-ounce can chili with beans**

**One 15-ounce can corn**

Dinner Party

# THE CANS FESTIVAL

Wondering what to do with your Y2K food stash? Host your own Cans Festival! This is a dinner party where everything served comes out of a can. Everything! And after you're done eating, you can enjoy hours of crafting with tin.

**MENU:**
First course: **Corn-a-Plenty Chowder**
Entrée: **Chili con Corne**
Side dish: canned green beans
Dessert: canned fruit cocktail
Beverage: can of soda or beer

# Chef Boyardee **Blitzkrieg** ✳

This is the perfect dish for the pasta lover who doesn't like grappling with terminology like *al dente* and *boiling water*. And if you've got a lot of people to feed, this pasta free–for–all is a no–hassle crowd pleaser. All kinds of pasta come together in a melting pot of noodley goodness mined with hot–dog grenades.

Open all the cans and mix with the hot dogs in a large, microwave-safe bowl.

Heat in the microwave oven on high until heated throughout, about 8 minutes. Serve hot.

**SERVES 8**

*You will need:*

**Six 15-ounce cans Chef Boyardee pasta (We recommend mini ravioli, Beefaroni, Cheesy Burger ravioli, lasagna, Twistaroni, and pepperoni Pizzazaroli)**

**4 hot dogs, sliced into bite-sized morsels**

# *Sloppy* José ✳

Sure, there's nothing wrong with a good ol' Sloppy Joe when you're hungry and you want a filling meal, pronto. But sometimes a man needs a little kick in his sandwich. By substituting canned chili for fresh ground beef, we've eliminated the pesky cooking aspect of this old favorite, without losing a single ounce of its manliness quotient. *¡Ay caramba!*

*You will need:*

**1 handful diced onions from the condiment bar**

**1 tablespoon butter, softened**

**One 15-ounce can no-bean chili con carne**

**4 packets taco sauce from the condiment bar**

**4 hamburger buns**

Toss the onions and butter in a microwave-safe bowl to combine. Heat in the microwave oven on high until the onions are translucent, about 2 minutes.

Add the chili and taco sauce and continue microwaving on high until heated throughout, 3–4 minutes longer.

Meanwhile, toast the hamburger buns in a toaster until golden brown.

Spoon the hot chili mixture onto the toasted bun bottoms, cover with the top buns, and serve.

**SERVES 4**

## MINI-MART ETIQUETTE

Whatever you do, never bring food purchased at one mini-mart into another mini-mart to heat up. This is the biggest faux pas one could make, alerting the staff that you are not only impolite, but an amateur. It could result in your being 86ed from the store, and you might sully your reputation around town. Treat them with politeness and courtesy, and your efforts will be rewarded threefold.

# The Tooth Grinder ✳ !

Grinder. Submarine sandwich. Hoagie. No matter what you call it, there's no denying the allure and practicality of the elongated sandwich. But let's face it: Sometimes you have to challenge yourself, and you'll be hard-pressed to find a greater test of your chewing skills than our Tooth Grinder. Piles of beef jerky and American cheese make a tasty and molar-wrenching meal. It's an exercise for your jaw, but not your pocketbook (unless, of course, you factor in the possible dental work).

*You will need:*

**1 packet mayonnaise from the condiment bar**

**1 packet mustard from the condiment bar**

**1 hot dog bun**

**3 assorted sticks jerky**

**2 slices American cheese**

**One ³/₄-ounce bag Funyuns**

**Italian dressing (optional)**

Spread the mayonnaise and mustard on the hot dog bun.

Pile on the jerky, cheese, and a handful of Funyuns.

If you like your grinder to have a little zing, add some Italian dressing.

Serve the grinder on a plate with the remaining Funyuns.

**SERVES 1**

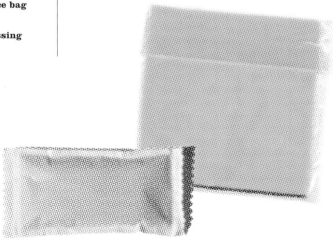

# *Low Rider* Lasagna

This spicy dish is as smooth as a ride in a cherried–out Impala. We've driven lasagna to new heights in this enchilada–ish casserole. It's better than boring old traditional lasagna, and there's no boiling required. Buckle up and take a little trip, take a little trip, take a little trip with me.

*You will need:*

**12 corn tortillas, torn into bite-sized pieces**

**One 15-ounce can pinto beans**

**One 15-ounce can corn**

**One 15-ounce can diced tomatoes**

**16 ounces Cheddar cheese, sliced or grated**

Preheat the oven to 350 degrees F.

Arrange half of the tortilla pieces in a greased 9-by-13-inch baking dish to cover the bottom. Top evenly with half each of the beans, corn, tomatoes, and cheese.

Layer the rest of the tortilla pieces on top and cover with the remaining beans, corn, tomatoes, and cheese.

Cover with aluminum foil and bake for 30 minutes. Remove the foil and continue to bake until the cheese begins to brown, about 15 minutes longer.

Eat hot, sitting on the hood of your Impala.

**SERVES 6**

# Chip Scramble

Chip, chip, hooray! This deceptively simple breakfast dish will have you kicking yourself, wondering why you didn't think of it first. Well, lucky for you, we did. Combining crushed chips and scrambled eggs allows you to get your crunch on, while rendering hash browns unnecessary. The best thing about this dish is that it can be tailor-made to suit even the pickiest little whipper-snapper's tastes. Substitute cheese puffs for a cheesy crunch, pork rinds for a ham-and-egg craving, or go South of the Border with tortilla chips. Lastly, say good-bye to salt shaker–induced wrist injuries, as the chips supply all the seasoning you need, and then some.

In a small bowl, beat together the eggs and milk.

Pour the egg mixture into a frying pan over medium heat and cook until the eggs are soft curds and opaque throughout. Remove from the heat.

With a knife, razor blade, nail clippers, or ice pick, poke a small hole in the top of the bag of chips.

Smash the chips to smithereens inside the bag (a rubber mallet or hammer works the best, but your hands will do just fine).

Pour the crushed chips into the eggs and mix until evenly distributed. Serve immediately.

**SERVES 2**

*You will need:*

**4 eggs**

**$^1/_4$ cup milk**

**One $2^3/_4$-ounce bag of potato chips, any flavor**

# Tuna on a *Cloud* ✳

Imagine an angel sleeping peacefully on a fluffy cloud. Now,
imagine that same serene scene, minus the angel and plus a fish.
A tuna fish. Tuna fish salad, actually. On closer inspection you
realize the cloud is really a buttery pillow of mashed potatoes.
Heavenly.

*You will need:*

**One 6-ounce can tuna**

**2 packets mayonnaise
from the condiment
bar**

**1 packet relish from
the condiment bar**

**1 1/3 cups water**

**1/2 cup milk**

**2 tablespoons butter**

**1 1/3 cups instant
mashed potato flakes**

**Salt and pepper**

In a small bowl, combine the tuna, mayonnaise, and relish.
Set aside.

In a microwave-safe bowl, combine the water, milk, and
butter and heat in the microwave oven on high until heated
throughout, about 2 minutes.

Stir the potato flakes into the milk mixture and season to
taste with salt and pepper.

Spoon the mashed potatoes onto a plate, top with the tuna
salad, and serve.

**SERVES 2 ANGELS**

Mini-Mart Craft Project

# YOUR OWN BEER COZY

Now that you're spending quite a bit of time at your local mini-mart, it's time to take the next step and actually buy a beer cozy. To distinguish your beer cozy from your friends' and family's cozies, decorate it in a manner that fits your style. For inspiration, look no further than the gumball-style machines in your mini-mart. They are full of stickers, rhinestone jewelry, and assorted plastic toys that will turn an ordinary beer cozy into a masterpiece that would make Martha Stewart green with envy.

# CORN DOG Kabobs

We know what you're thinking: "Corn dogs could not be more delicious than they already are. And they come on a stick as it is. How could this be improved upon?" It can't—that much is true. We don't want to alter this perfect food; we just want to squeeze in a side dish. Bite–sized chunks of corn dogs cozy up next to golden Tater Tots to make a complete meal on a stick.

Preheat the oven to 350 degrees F.

Place the corn dogs and Tater Tots on an ungreased baking sheet.

Bake for 9 minutes, then flip the dogs and tots and bake for about 9 minutes longer, or until both the corn dogs and potatoes are golden brown.

Remove the corn dogs from their sticks and cut into 1-inch pieces. (Eat the rounded ends.) Thread the Tater Tots and corn dog pieces onto the empty corn dog sticks.

Garnish with ketchup and mustard and enjoy pups and tots on a stick.

**SERVES 4**

*You will need:*

**4 frozen corn dogs**

**24 frozen Tater Tots**

**2 packets ketchup from the condiment bar**

**2 packets mustard from the condiment bar**

## MINI-MART TRIVIA

There are approximately 125,000 convenience stores in the United States. Of those, about 12,800 are in the biggest and baddest state in the union, Texas, making it the home to the most mini-marts in the United States.

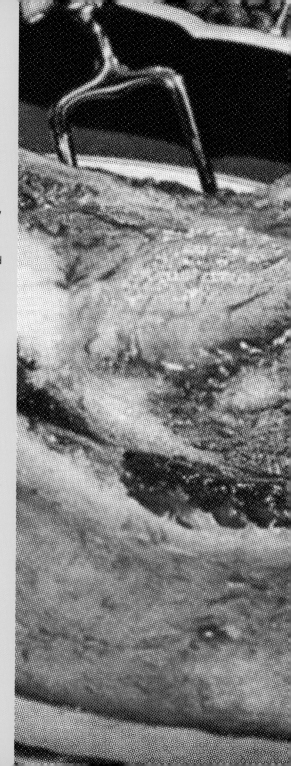

Dinner Party

# RETRO VIVA

Other than the '80s, '70s, and '60s, no
other decade is more in style right now
than the '50s. Why not throw a dinner
party honoring the era when children
were polite, adults were repressed, and
it was still okay to eat five servings of
red meat a day, Daddy-O.

**MENU:**

First course: **Sardines Rockefeller**

Entrée: **SPAM Wellington**

Side dish: **Ramen Romanoff**

Dessert: **Tapioca Brulée**

Beverage: **The Hula Hoop**

# Salami Goulash ✳ !

This Hungarian specialty is cooked many different ways, but to date, no varieties have included salami. And if that wasn't enough, previously all goulashes we've seen have included persnickety and potentially volatile spices. Yet again, we scoff in the face of tradition and serve up a warm and hearty stew minus paprika, but plus pizzazz.

Toss together the onions and butter in a large microwave-safe bowl and heat in the microwave oven on high for 2 minutes, or until the onions are translucent.

Add the beef broth, tomato juice, and garlic powder and heat on high for 5 minutes longer, or until heated throughout.

Add the green beans, salami, and sour cream. Stir and heat for about 2 minutes longer. Season to taste with salt and pepper.

Dig out your grandma's Hungarian polka records and enjoy!

**SERVES 4**

*You will need:*

**1 handful diced onions from the condiment bar**

**1 tablespoon butter, softened**

**One 15-ounce can beef broth**

**1 cup tomato juice**

**$1/_2$ teaspoon garlic powder**

**One 14$1/_2$-ounce can cut green beans**

**8 ounces salami, julienned**

**$1/_2$ cup sour cream**

**Salt and pepper**

# 3

## Beverages

Classy folks the world over treat the art of beverage creation and consumption as almost a religion. Having a drink is more, so much more, than just whetting your whistle. It is about coming together socially, setting aside our differences and regrets and washing them clean with the perfect combination of flavors riding a delicious wave down the throat. What follows are potions to make the most monumental of toasts with, to soothe the saddest of souls with, to heal the most broken of hearts with. The elixirs of your dreams, and they're no farther than your very own mini-mart.

# The Brain Drain

This drink will take you back to your younger days before you figured out that maybe, just maybe, lots of sugar mixed with lots of alcohol isn't the greatest combination ever. Frozen slushee and grain alcohol mix to create this simple yet intoxicating quencher. It's the adult Slurpee, or at least the "I just turned legal yesterday" Slurpee. It's ideal for when you're running low on time and energy, but still crave a refreshing adult beverage. When the headache hits you, you won't know if it's from the grain alcohol or the ice-cold slush.

Fill the cup with slushee, leaving a little room for the alcohol.

Add the good stuff, stir, and enjoy.

**INTOXICATES 1**

*You will need:*

**20-ounce frozen slushee drink, any flavor**

**2 ounces grain alcohol**

## SUCKS FOR YOU

Most of the beverages in this chapter contain alcohol, and are for adults only. So if you're under the legal drinking age, well, that sucks for you. We're also operating on the assumption that you are fortunate enough to live in a state where it's legal to sell alcohol in mini-marts. And again, if you don't, well, that sucks for you.

Unfortunately, because it is illegal to have any kind of open containers with alcohol in them in public, none of the alcoholic beverages in this chapter can be made in-store, unless you want to risk going to jail for a little convenience, which the authors don't recommend—that would really suck.

# *Liquid* Ricky Martin

This peppy beverage has lots of kick and just the right amount of fluff to keep it in the Top Ten for months. Coffee, cocoa, and whipped cream join forces with Puerto Rican rum to make this eye–opener more than just a guilty pleasure. You'll be hitting all the high notes with a head that's creamy and a body that's the color of mocha. It's so dangerously delicious, you'll be livin' *la vida loca.*

*You will need:*

**8 ounces hot brewed coffee**

**One 1 1/4-ounce packet hot cocoa mix**

**1 1/2 ounces Puerto Rican rum**

**Can of whipped cream**

Mix the coffee and cocoa in a 16-ounce cup and stir until the cocoa is dissolved.

Add the rum and top with a tower of whipped cream. Sip and spin.

**SERVES 1**

## UNCLE JOHNNY'S MINI-MART HISTORY MINUTE

The first twenty-four-hour mini-mart was a 7-Eleven in Austin, Texas. One night in 1962, the store was so busy after a University of Texas football game that it never closed its doors that fateful Saturday night, and soon thereafter it was open twenty-four hours a day, seven days a week.

# The **AMBULANCE** Chaser ✳ !

For the soccer mom who doesn't have a minute to catch a breath, much less make a well–rounded meal, this satisfying drink, made from instant soup and vitamin supplements, is a gift from god. Kill two birds with one stone: hunger and scurvy. In about the time it takes to strap little Jimmy into the car seat, you could have a delicious and nutritious lunch that you can eat with one hand. What you do with the other hand is up to you.

*You will need:*

**One 10³/₄-ounce bottle of Campbell's Soup at Hand (we recommend creamy tomato)**

**1 packet lemon-lime or orange-flavored Emer'gen-C**

Remove the plastic cap and metal lid from the soup.

Heat the soup in the microwave oven for 1¹/₂ minutes, or until heated throughout.

Add the Emer'gen-C, stir, and replace the plastic cap.

**SERVES 1**

# The *Hula Hoop*

This is the drink version of a vintage 1952 kitchenette; it's simple, colorful, and fun. One sip of this concoction, and you'll find yourself transported to the beach, breeze blowing through your hair, not a care in the world. So kick off your shoes, swing your hips, and let the tropical flavor spin you round and round. If you start getting dizzy, though, slow it down; you don't want this punch to knock you silly.

Mix the fruit punch and rum in a large punch bowl. Ladle in small cups, to order.

**SERVES 12**

**Variation: The Wussy Hoop**
*Substitute lemonade for the rum.*

*You will need:*

**6 cups fruit punch**

**1 cup light rum**

# The **Rabid Dog**!

This is a fun drink that will freak out your friends. By mixing Mad Dog 20/20 with a handful of free creamer packets, you'll get a concoction that looks like the mouth of a golden retriever with a full-blown case of rabies, and a taste that's even better! Not only that, but we promise it will make you no sicker than if you drank only the Mad Dog.

*You will need:*

**1 bottle Mad Dog 20/20 Orange Jubilee**

**3 creamer packets from the condiment bar**

Remove the cap and take a pull off the Mad Dog to make room for the creamers.

Add the creamers, re-cap, and shake. Pour into 4 Collins glasses and serve.

**SERVES 4 (LIMIT 1 PER PERSON! ARF!)**

Dinner Party

# HALLOWEEN FEAST

Halloween is the ultimate mini-mart holiday, as the store itself is chock-full of tricks and treats. If you're feeling too old to go out begging for candy, but still want to honor this sugar-riffic holiday, why not host a dinner party for your favorite ghouls and goblins?

**MENU:**

First course: **Saucy Devils**
Entrée: **Bat out of Hell Meatloaf**
Dessert: **Creamed Candy Corn**
Beverage: **The Rabid Dog**

# Quick Cheese Tricks

## Cheese SMOOTHIE !

Hear Ye! Hear Ye! We declare that cheese is no longer restricted to solid form! If you're as fond of dairy as we are, you too have considered ways in which you could not only eat, but also drink or perhaps even inhale, cheese. With our tantalizing cheese smoothie, we liquefy our favorite dairy delight into a frothy and filling masterpiece.

*You will need:*

**1 cup milk**

**¹/₄ cup cottage cheese**

**¹/₄ cup Cheez Whiz**

**¹/₄ cup crushed ice**

Combine all the ingredients in a blender and blend on high for about 30 seconds, or until frothy.

**SERVES 1**

### Variation: Wussy Smoothie

*Substitute 3 tablespoons frozen lemonade concentrate for the Cheez Whiz to create a liquid lemon cheesecake.*

## MINI-MART TRIVIA

One out of nine people in the United States will eat a hot dog at a Circle K store this year.

# The **Mickey Rourke**

These days, to be "street" is to be cool. And what says "street" more than a cold (or not) forty ounces of malt liquor? Nothing, that's what. But, then again, sometimes you want something a little less rough around the edges. You want something smooth (like Mickey Rourke in *9 1/2 Weeks*), but you don't want to sacrifice your hard-earned street cred (like Mickey Rourke in *Harley Davidson and the Marlboro Man*). Well, fret no more, punk, because once the strawberry soda hits the malt liquor and that sip hits your lips, you'll find your hair slicking back on its own.

*You will need:*

**One 40-ounce bottle Mickey's malt liquor**

**One 12-ounce can strawberry soda**

Fill a Collins glass three-quarters full with the Mickey's. Top with the strawberry soda and serve.

**SERVES 4**

**Variation: The Mickey Pourke !**
*Same ingredients, garnished with Vienna sausages.*

Mini-Mart Craft Project

# JELL-O FINGER PAINTING

Are you looking for an activity to occupy your children while you're busy cooking the Cans Festival (page 53) for your friends? Or perhaps you fancy yourself an amateur Van Gogh. It's time to try finger painting with Jell-O. Just pick out some colors you like, mix the powder with a small amount of water, and voilà, you've got a vivid palette with which to paint many a masterpiece.

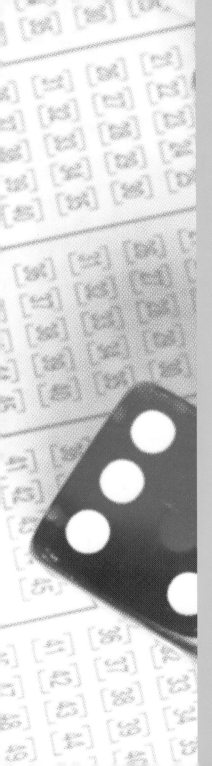

## MINI-MART ETIQUETTE

One of the many perks of shopping at a mini-mart is that you have the option to gamble while you shop. Most stores offer a wide variety of scratch-offs, lotto, and keno games. If baby needs a new pair of shoes, go ahead and do a little gambling, but remember, there are people in the store who are doing some serious shopping and you don't want to stall them by hogging the counter at checkout time. Decide in advance which scratch-offs you want; know what lotto numbers you are going to pick; and for the love of god, once you've purchased your tickets, step aside to scratch off your scratch-off so the next customer can be on their way as well. Clerks and fellow customers alike will appreciate your considerate efforts.

## NEW PRODUCTS

You may think you are very well acquainted with the entire stock of your mini-mart, but the snack industry is always pumping out new and tasty products. Keep your peepers open and observe the shelves with a fresh eye. Hiding behind that can of chili may be some exciting new product you've never even heard of before.

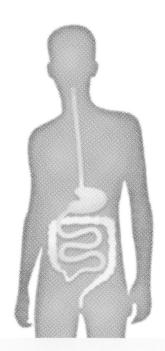

# The *Pink of Health* !

These days, the health industry is so aggressive in its promotion of new medications and remedies that it is pushing medicine to cure aches before they even hit your weary bones. Heartburn medicine *before* you have heartburn? What? Rather than grumble, we decided to jump on the bandwagon. Here is a breakthrough beverage that delivers both the cause of and the cure for the hangover. Smirnoff Ice and Pepto-Bismol combine to cure what ails you in this experimental, groundbreaking cocktail. Here's to your health!

*You will need:*

**One 24-ounce bottle Smirnoff Ice**

**¼ cup Pepto-Bismol**

**Ice cubes**

Pour the Smirnoff Ice into two glasses filled with ice.

Add the Pepto-Bismol, stir, and enjoy.

**CURES 2**

# Thousand Island **Iced Tea** !

Long Island Iced Tea, Blue Hawaiian, Sex on the Beach . . . so many tropical drinks, all with oodles of liquor, but nothing to stick to your ribs. Where is the drink that can quench your thirst and satisfy your hunger at the same time? Here it is, friend: the only drink ever made featuring mayonnaise as an ingredient. This is a cocktail tailor made for the kind of person who likes double special sauce on their burgers, or the person who by-passes the ketchup when the french fries arrive and goes straight for the mayo. Plus, this drink comes with the built–in inebriation blocker—it's simply too filling and rich to drink more than one.

*You will need:*

**Ice cubes**

**$1\frac{1}{2}$ ounces rum**

**$\frac{3}{4}$ ounce vodka**

**$\frac{3}{4}$ ounce gin**

**$\frac{3}{4}$ ounce Triple Sec**

**1 packet mayonnaise from the condiment bar**

**1 packet ketchup from the condiment bar**

Fill a pint glass with ice and add the rum, vodka, gin, and Triple Sec.

Add the mayonnaise and ketchup and stir. Bottoms up!

**SERVES 1**

### Variation: No Man's Island Ice Tea

*Substitute $\frac{1}{4}$ cup orange juice, $\frac{3}{4}$ ounce half-and-half, and $\frac{1}{2}$ teaspoon grenadine for the mayonnaise and ketchup if you're not man enough for a real drink.*

# The *Laura Palmer*

For those of you fortunate enough never to have waited on tables in your life, you might not know that the Arnold Palmer is the favored lunchtime beverage of America's office workforce. But once that smug, overweight businessman sets down his cell phone to reply to your confused stare and your "A what, what?" with a curt "Half lemonade, half iced tea" before returning to his mobile conference call, it will forever be burned into your memory. The Arnold Palmer is fine, but it's a little boring for our tastes, so we decided to spike it à la David Lynch. Now, we know it's fiction, but we imagine that before young Miss Laura Palmer met her fate, she would while away her afternoons in Twin Peaks drinking something more befitting her devil–may–care lifestyle. Even the Log Lady would set down her wooden companion to grab hold of one of these babies.

Fill two Collins glasses with ice and fill each with half Hard Lemonade and half Hard Iced Tea.

Stir and enjoy while discussing your favorite Twin Peaks character.

**SERVES 2**

*You will need:*

**One 11-ounce bottle Mike's Hard Lemonade**

**One 11-ounce bottle Mike's Hard Iced Tea**

# MINI-MARTS ON THE BIG SCREEN

Mini-marts have played a role not only in everyone's lives, but also in Hollywood. Some memorable mini-mart moments include the 1994 comedy *Clerks*, the under-appreciated 1981 sit-com *Open All Night,* and the rarely-seen adult movie *Convenience Store Girls*.

4

Desserts

A mini-mart gourmet meal without dessert is a complete facade. It's like a train without a caboose. It's like a TV dinner without the TV, or maybe with really bad reception and no remote. The dessert is like the treasure at the end of a long, tasty treasure hunt. Have you ever heard anyone remark, "Save room for toast"? No, you haven't, and if you're going to hit the brakes on something that is as delicious as one of our entrées, than it had better damn well be worth it.

The number of mini-mart dessert options is so vast, it almost warrants its own book. We could write chapters on the merits of Tapioca Brûlée (page 100), or that underwater wonderland, the Aquarium (page 99), but we have already taken up enough of your time, time that could have been spent gorging. So save a little room, get your sweet tooth on, and let's go.

# **HO** Cakes ✳

There's nothing quite as impressive as a tray of assorted tiny desserts. Here we offer our version of pétits fours made from a variety of Hostess Cakes. These little treats are as easy as a cheap date. It's haute cuisine minus the baking and plus a lengthy shelf life. Best of all, they're ho–made.

*You will need:*

**5 packages assorted Hostess Cakes (we recommend Twinkies, Ho Hos, Zingers, Ding Dongs, and Suzy Qs)**

**Can of whipped cream**

**18 whole almonds**

With a large knife, slice the ends off of the cakes and eat them.

Cut each cake into squares (you should get 2 squares out of each Twinkie-shaped cake and 1 out of each Ding-Dong shaped cake).

Top each with a dab of whipped cream and an almond.

Arrange on a tray and serve.

**SERVES 4**

# MINI-MART TRIVIA

Up until 1946, 7-Eleven stores used to be called "Tote'm" stores because customers "tote'd" away their haul.

# *Creamed* Candy Corn ✳

One of the foulest foods to ever find its way into a can is the dreaded creamed corn. What we have here is a complete overhaul of that side dish that will leave a sweet taste in your mouth. Butterscotch topping and candy corn unite for the first (and probably the last) time to create a welcome addition to ice cream, graham crackers, or pound cake.

*You will need:*

**One 12¼-ounce jar butterscotch topping**

**½ cup candy corn**

Heat the jar of butterscotch topping in the microwave for 30 seconds. Pour the butterscotch topping into a small bowl and stir in the candy corn.

Scoop onto ice cream, cake, crackers, or anything that needs a little boost of corny sweetness and serve immediately.

**SERVES 4**

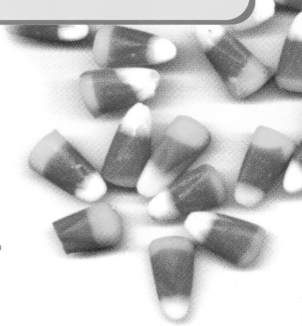

Mini-Mart Craft Project

## ICE CREAM CONE SCULPTURE

Of all the things available to an artist in the mini-mart, we see the most potential in a pack of sugar ice cream cones. Use them to make Madonna bras, fake chins, party hats, or miniature orange safety cones.

# Banana *Nicole Smith* *

You'll be laughing all the way to the bank with this boda-cious beauty. Like our southern belle, this sundae is rich and easy. Two bountiful scoops of vanilla ice cream and a ton of fat gams (oops—grams) make this baby hard to resist, even to the crotchety old man who's been set in his ways since his early seventies.

Divide the ice cream into 2 double D-sized scoops and place in a shallow, oval serving dish.

Cover the ice cream liberally with whipped cream.

Top with the Laffy Taffy and cherries and serve.

**SERVES A PAIR**

You will need:

**1 pint vanilla ice cream**

**Can of whipped cream**

**6 banana-flavored Laffy Taffy candies**

**2 maraschino cherries**

# Sugar **Shingles**

Peel off a piece from the house of tastiness. Chocolate, butter, and sugar join forces with saltine crackers to create this sweet–and–salty decadent dessert. It may look like a piece of roofing material, but it tastes like heaven.

*You will need:*

$^1/_2$ **cup (1 stick) butter**

**1 cup sugar**

**Four 1.55-ounce chocolate bars**

**40 saltines crackers**

Preheat the oven to 300 degrees F.

Place the butter in a small microwave-safe bowl and heat in the microwave oven on high for 1 minute, or until the butter is melted.

Add the sugar to the butter and stir until dissolved.

Break the chocolate bars into small pieces and place in another small microwave-safe bowl. Heat in the microwave oven on high for 2 minutes, or until the chocolate is melted.

Place the crackers on an ungreased baking sheet and spread the butter and sugar mixture on top. Spoon the melted chocolate over the buttered crackers.

Bake for 30 minutes. Let cool for 15 minutes before serving.

**SERVES 8**

# FRESH STOCK IS AT THE BACK OF THE ROW

Now, we realize that pretty much everything in the mini-mart has a minimum shelf life of twelve years. Still, there's nothing finer than a new bag of chips, fresh off the Frito-Lay assembly line. Grab the item that is farthest from your reach to ensure the highest quality and freshest flavor.

# Rashcakes

If you've got an itch for something sweet and cakey, this quick and simple dish will help you scratch it. Traditional pancakes and red hot candies will get your day started off on the right foot, even if you woke up on the wrong side of the bed. There's no need for syrup, because your blast of sweetness is built right into the cake. These little sizzlers aren't just for breakfast either, unless you always limit your sweetest snacks for the early morning hours. As an added bonus, you get cinnamon breath to boot. So say good–bye to your toothbrush and hello to your frying pan.

*You will need:*

**2 cups original Bisquick**

**1 cup milk**

**2 eggs**

**One 2-ounce box Hot Tamales candies, each candy cut in half**

**1 tablespoon melted butter**

In a large bowl, stir together the Bisquick, milk, and eggs.

Cut the Hot Tamales in half.

Preheat a nonstick frying pan or griddle until hot. Brush with a little of the melted butter. Slowly ladle a scant $1/4$ cup batter into the pan. Ladle in more batter to make as many pancakes as you can without letting them touch.

Tuck 12 Hot Tamales halves into each pancake. Cook the pancakes until they begin to bubble, the edges begin to dry, and the bottoms are golden brown, about 2 minutes. Flip with a spatula and continue cooking until the second side is golden brown, about 1 minute longer. Repeat with the remaining butter, batter, and Hot Tamales.

Serve with the ointment of your choice.

**SERVES 4**

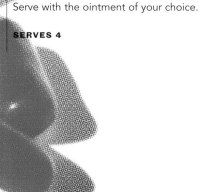

# *Ice Cream* Parfait for a Gang

This Oreo–crusted ice cream cake is better than a diamond crusted gold chain. Big enough for two gangs, and sweet enough for the ladies, we're sure they'd all declare a truce if they met over a mound of this fantastic frozen treat.

*You will need:*

**Half-gallon ice cream, any flavor**

**32 Oreo cookies**

**$1/_4$ cup melted butter**

**$7^1/_4$-ounce bottle Magic Shell chocolate sauce**

Take the ice cream out of the freezer to soften.

Dump the Oreos into a large bowl and break them up into small pieces. Add the melted butter and stir.

Pour the Oreo mixture into a greased 9-by-13-inch dish. Place in the freezer for 20 minutes.

Spread the softened ice cream on top of the Oreo crust. Top with the entire bottle of Magic Shell and return to the freezer until the ice cream is firm again, about 30 minutes. Cut into squares and serve.

**SERVES 1 GANG**

Dinner Party

# FIESTA FEED

Can't make it to Cancun for your annual vacation? No problemo! Just throw on a poncho and head down to your local mini-mart and create a feast for your amigos, Mexican-style.

**MENU:**

First course: **Pigs in a Poncho**

Entrée: **Low Rider Lasagna**

Dessert: **Rashcakes**

Beverage: **Liquid Ricky Martin**

# EATING IN YOUR CAR

The authors don't like to eat and drive. We think it's slightly dangerous, and frankly, we're usually too engrossed in our food to even scratch our bums, let alone operate a vehicle. That said, we do think that a car is an excellent place to dine, just so long as it's not moving. There are some preparations one can make to ensure an enjoyable vehicular dining experience:

1.  **You can never have too many napkins.** Always keep plenty of napkins in the glove box. These are available for free in your mini-mart near the hot dog fixins.

2.  **Cup holders are a must.** If your car doesn't already have them, invest in a portable plastic set. They will pay for themselves in money saved not dry cleaning ketchup off of your favorite white pantsuit.

3.  **Condiments are free and last forever.** Keep extra condiment packets in the glove box. You'll probably be dining in the mini-mart parking lot most of the time, but for those evenings when you feel like watching the sunset from say, a K-Mart parking lot, an extra hit of mustard can really come in handy.

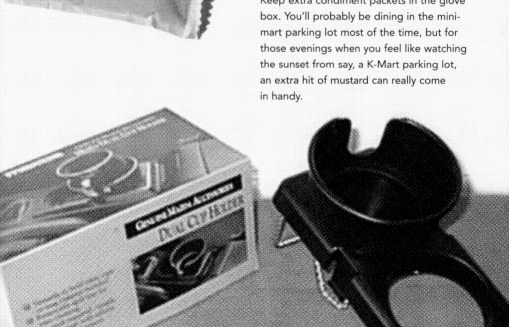

# The Aquarium

It is true that much has been done with Jell-O, but this dessert is truly special. The gummy fish swimming happily in a delicious sea of blue will elicit a smile even from those who are always bitching about the questionable animal parts that go into making gelatin such a wonderfully jiggly experience. So forget about adding boring old bananas or grapes to your Jell-O, and let's go fishin'.

Bring 4 cups of water to a boil in a large saucepan.

In a large, clear glass bowl, stir together the gelatin and boiling water until no blue grains are visible.

Add 4 cups cold water and stir to mix well.

Refrigerate for 1 hour, or until semi-thick, and then stir in the gummy fish.

Refrigerate until firm, about 2 hours longer. Serve cold.

**SERVES 8**

**Variation: The Extreme Aquarium !**
*For a more authentic aquarium experience, substitute sardines for the gummy fish.*

*You will need:*

**8 cups water**

**One 12-ounce package Berry Blue Jell-O**

**One 8-ounce package Snak Stop Ju Ju Fish or comparable gummy marine life**

## MINI-MART ETIQUETTE

We all have our own sense of style. Your mini-mart clerk understands that as well as anyone. That said, there are a few items that should never, under any circumstances, be worn into a convenience store. These include, but are not limited to: ski masks, panty hose worn over the face, and bandanas of any color, worn bandit-style.

# Tapioca **Brûlée**

Here you get all the danger and awe of crème brûlée without the fuss. Once your friends are mesmerized by the open flame dancing around this creamy dessert, they won't even notice that it is just a glorified bowl of tapioca pudding. Please do not attempt this dessert without a fire extinguisher and escape route handy.

*You will need:*

**One 6-pack Jell-O Tapioca Snacks**

**³/₄ cup brown sugar**

**3 tablespoons 151-proof rum**

Preheat the broiler.

Spoon the tapioca into 3 separate heatproof bowls (2 snacks per each bowl).

Sprinkle the brown sugar evenly over the top of the tapioca in each bowl.

Place the bowls on a baking sheet and slip under the broiler for 1 minute, or until the sugar is melted and the top is slightly browned.

Drizzle 1 tablespoon of rum over the top of each browned tapioca.

With a match or lighter, set the tapioca ablaze. After the flames burn out, serve immediately.

**SERVES 3**

**Variation: Tapioca Brown**
*Ignore all the steps concerning rum and fire.*

# Twinkie *Surprise*

**This wonderful dessert allows you to use your own creative nature to add a personal touch to the famous treat that has been rotting teeth for decades. By hollowing out the cream filling, you make room for fun. The only limit to this crowd pleaser is your imagination. It's like Russian roulette, but with a happy ending.**

Remove the plastic wrap from Twinkies and set them side by side on a large plate.

Using a wide straw, suck the cream from the three cream holes in the bottom of one of the Twinkies. Blow out or swallow the creamy filling. Poke a hole with said straw in one end of the Twinkie and suck and spit (or eat) again until you can blow into the straw and feel air coming through all of the bottom cream holes. Repeat with each Twinkie.

To fill the Twinkies, using a small funnel, carefully pour liquid fillings, if any, into each empty hole. For small candies, or other bits, just shove them up the holes. For Slurpee filling, place the end hole under the tap and pull the lever. (Some stores may frown on this.)

**SERVES 5**

*You will need:*

**10 Twinkies**

**Fillings of your choice (we suggest chocolate sauce, cherry Slurpee, M&M's, bacon, etc.)**

# The **Dirtbag**

By adding one simple ingredient to Cool Whip, you have a dessert that is ready to serve in mere seconds. You'll be whipped into a frenzy with this chocolate mousse imitation.

*You will need:*

**One 8-ounce bucket of Cool Whip**

**Two 1-ounce packets hot cocoa**

If necessary, defrost the Cool Whip in the refrigerator until soft.

Spoon the Cool Whip into a large bowl.

Add the cocoa and stir until the two become one.

**SERVES 6**

**Variation: The Fruit Bag**

*Substitute 8 ounces of any fruit-flavored yogurt for the cocoa.*

## UNCLE JOHNNY'S MINI-MART HISTORY MINUTE

During the 1920s, mobile convenience stores called "motorterias" along with drive-in markets allowed consumers to purchase their goods without getting out of their vehicles.

# *Peanut Butter* Bombs ✳

These nutty little grenades are the perfect treat for anyone who prefers cookie dough to actual cookies. By microwaving instead of baking, we ensure that there's no way to make them too hard or crispy. Mostly you're just heating up the dough and fixing it into a neat, easily transportable shape.

*You will need:*

**¹/₂ cup (1 stick) butter, softened**

**³/₄ cup brown sugar**

**¹/₄ cup granulated sugar**

**¹/₂ cup chunky peanut butter**

**1 egg**

**1¹/₂ cups flour**

**¹/₄ teaspoon salt**

**¹/₄ teaspoon baking soda**

In a large bowl, beat together the butter, brown sugar, granulated sugar, and peanut butter until smooth. Beat in the egg.

Add the flour, salt, and baking soda and stir to mix well.

Roll the dough into 1-inch balls. Place on a sheet of waxed paper and flatten with a fork.

Cook in the microwave oven on high for about 3 minutes, or until firm. Let cool and serve.

**SERVES 6**

# Lower the Bar Cookies

Brownies are good for two reasons. One is because they are chocolate, obviously. The second reason is the dense, gooey texture that makes them melt in you mouth. Recently, a scientist in our mini–mart laboratory, Madame J, discovered a way to tweak the traditional brownie flavor, for those folks who tire of chocolate,* but not the brownie texture. Pick any flavor cake mix your heart desires (lemon, strawberry, cherry chip), follow our directions, and prepare your mouth for a flavorful, flat, square of brownielike cakey cookie.

Preheat the oven to 350 degrees F.

In a large bowl, beat together the cake mix, water, vegetable oil, and eggs until the batter is smooth.

Pour the batter into a greased 11-by-7-inch baking pan.

Bake until a toothpick inserted into the middle of the cake comes out clean, 40–45 minutes.

Let cool for 20 minutes. Cut into 24 squares and serve.

**SERVES 12**

*We hear that nonchocolate lovers exist, but aren't entirely sure this can be proven.

*You will need:*

**One 18 1/4-ounce box cake mix, any flavor**

**1/4 cup water**

**1/3 cup vegetable oil**

**2 eggs**

# *Index*

# *Mini-Mart* Table of Equivalents and Substitutions

| | |
|---:|:---|
| freshly squeezed lime juice | = Mountain Dew |
| 1 cup buttermilk | = 15 creamer packets + 1 pat butter |
| 1 bottle of champagne | = 1 bottle Mad Dog + food coloring |
| bread crumbs | = crushed potato chips |
| 1 cup tomato sauce | = $1/2$ cup water + $1/2$ cup ketchup |
| 1 bunch of fresh mint | = 1 plug wintergreen flavored chew |
| capers | = pickle relish from condiment bar |
| 1 teaspoon aoili | = 1 packet of mayo |
| 1 wheel of brie | = 1 brick of Velveeta left out overnight to form a skin |
| 1 plate of antipasti | = 4 Slim Jim snack packs + pickles from condiment bar |
| 2 scratch-its + 1 six pack + 1 Trojan Horse | = Set for the Night |